Jaclyn Leigh Young

INSIGHTS
from the
CURB

Trilogy Christian Publishers

A Wholly Owned Subsidiary of Trinity Broadcasting Network
2442 Michelle Drive
Tustin, CA 92780

Rights Department, 2442 Michelle Drive, Tustin, CA 92780.

Trilogy Christian Publishing/TBN and colophon are trademarks of
Trinity Broadcasting Network.

For information about special discounts for bulk purchases, please
contact Trilogy Christian Publishing.

Manufactured in the United States of America
10 9 8 7 6 5 4 3 2 1
Library of Congress Cataloging-in-Publication Data is available.
ISBN: 978-1-63769-216-5
E-ISBN: 978-1-63769-217-2

***Dedicated to Grandmother Annie,**
*Who cultivated my ambition for writing, enhanced my imagination,
and who taught me how to live out and love God's Word.*

FOREWORD

Our friend Jaclyn is a real-life hero and overcomer! She has faced suffering head-on and emerged glowing with joy! If you are battling with anxiety, fear, or trials, you need these beautiful words she has written to lead you to the feet of Jesus. Her inspiring 30-day devotional will give you hope and help you make sense of life's most uncertain days. Jaclyn is a treasure and her gift of communicating the promises of Jesus will change your life today and forever!

Linda and Jen Barrick
Hope Out Loud Ministries

TABLE OF CONTENTS

Day 1: Come, Taste, and See! 1

Day 2: Who is God to Me? 3

Day 3: What is a Friend 5

Day 4: No Sweeter Place to Be 7

Day 5: Joy That Never Dies 9

Day 6: Gratitude Leads to True Godliness 11

Day 7: What's so Great About Normal? 13

Day 8: When I Run, I Feel His Pleasure 15

Day 9: He Grants Purpose 17

Day 10: In His Arms You Can Rest 19

Day 11: God's Outcomes are Better Than Our Suggestions 21

Day 12: What God Ordains is Always Good 23

Day 13: When We Fall, He Doesn't Leave Us There 25

Day 14: The Lord Remembers His Beloved 27

Day 15: What Could Be Better? 29

Day 16: The Two Greatest Words to Hear 31

Day 17: God is Strong Enough to Carry You 33

Day 18: A Place to Belong 35

Day 19: God Will Use Great Trials for Great Victories 37

Day 20: He Only Gives the Best 39

Day 21: It's Not About Us 41

Day 22: What Are You Here For? 43

Day 23: Do We Even Matter? 45

Day 24: Fear Has No Hold 47

Day 25: As Christians, We Have the Ultimate Duty 49

Day 26: He Doesn't Make Mistakes 51

Day 27: Grace, Unending Grace! 53

Day 28: He Holds Us by the Strength of His Hand 55

Day 29: Total Surrender 57

Day 30: All Creatures, Praise His Name! 59

Dear Reader,

Do you like stories or films that involve the characters finding some form of buried treasure? They seem to spend much time studying the maps and clues that lead to the desired riches. In the end, they are filled with satisfaction and content by their discoveries. Bad guys disappear, and the good guys relish in the joy of their changed lives. This might be far-fetched, I think there are times in our life when we feel like we have to piece our path on our own. It isn't until we recognize that God has revealed such lasting riches through His Word. Most view the Bible as the map to a "good life." While it does direct and teach us how to live godly lives, I see Scripture as the treasure trove of Who God is and His rich love for us. No earthly treasure or possession can ever match that reality!

In this little book, Insights from the Curb, we are going to barely scratch the surface of some of these truths. Whether you go through this on your own, or you read it surrounded by your family, I pray that you will take time to dive deeper into the discovery of these truths. Some of these concepts may seem repetitive, but I don't believe one can look at the same situation through the same lens. As a woman with Cerebral Palsy, I guess you could say that Suffering is a close acquaintance of mine. Yet so is Joy! I think of the apostle Paul who was well-acquainted with the troubles of this sinful world. Like Paul, I am thankful that Jesus knows exactly how we feel in grief, but He also shares in our triumphs. As the writer of Hebrews says, "For we do not have a high priest who is unable to sympathize with our weaknesses, but one who has been tempted as we are, yet without sin. Let us then with confidence draw near to the throne of grace, that we may receive mercy and find grace to help in time of need." (Hebrews 4:15-16, ESV). Friend, as this book has been written over the course of several years, you have been prayed for. As you go through the valleys of life, or on the mountain top, may the peace and hope of our Lord Jesus Christ guide your steps. May His grace comfort and strengthen you as you run the Race well until the Day when He calls His children Home...Oh what a Day that will be!

Blessings in His Grace,
Jaclyn

Day 1:
Come, Taste, and See!

"This poor man cried, and the LORD him and saved him of all his troubles. The angel of the LORD encamps around those who fear him and delivers them. Oh, taste and see that the LORD is good! Blessed is the man who takes refuge in him!"

Psalm 34:6-8 (ESV)

"Oh, taste and see that the LORD is good!" This is one of the most beloved phrases in all of Scripture, and rightfully so! In context, David is writing this as a song of praise to God for delivering him from king Achish, king of Gath, (1 Samuel 21:10-15, ESV). Once David escaped from Gath, he gave thanks to God for keeping him from harm, and David proclaims his gratitude by telling the Lord how good He is. I imagine that if he weren't on the run, David would be shouting this great declaration from the mountain tops! Instead, he writes it as a hymn, asking the congregation to praise the Lord Most High with him! In the same way, we as believers should approach God with such gratitude. God always deserves our uttermost praise whether we're deep in the valley, or high on the hilltop! Like David, we should be constantly seeking to tell the Lord what amazing works He's doing in our lives.

Though, we shouldn't pretend that praising God in the midst of temptation and hardship is easy. In fact, it's probably the most difficult part of the trial. We see in many of the Psalms that even David sometimes struggles with giving God glory, as we do...We so often seek the praise of others, and it can be a struggle to let go of that sinful motive. Yet, we gain an abundance in grace once we view God as the only One worthy of our worship! Essentially, we can in fact "taste and see that the LORD is good" in any circumstance that comes into our lives and to fear Him. The term "fear" used in this context as well as many other passages, is referring to our obedience and reverence to God. So, through our lives when we fear God, we are ultimately being obedient to His ways and acknowledge Who He is as God! As we seek to praise God in whatever circumstances, we can always, "taste and see that the LORD is good!"

Day 2:
Who is God to Me?

"The LORD is my light and my salvation; whom shall I fear? The LORD is the stronghold of my life; of whom shall I be afraid? When evildoers assail me to eat up my flesh, my adversaries and foes, it is they who stumble and fall. Though an army encamp against me, my heart shall not fear; though war arise against me, yet I will be confident."

Psalms 27:1-3 (ESV)

What is it that you fear? Is it fear of not having stability, health, money, shelter, food? Fear of not being loved and accepted by others? Maybe even fear of the future and all of the unknowns that are ahead? The list never ends! However, in this passage, David praises God as, "the light," recognizing Him as the One Who guides His People through the joyous and the doubtful times. David also refers to God as his, "salvation," confirming that God has indeed saved him from trouble. David wants to encourage us that because God our Light and Salvation, we don't have to be afraid of whatever happens in life. Now, and in every situation. The Lord was with David while he was afraid, and reminded him that when in God's presence, there is no room for fear!

Though overcoming fear can seem nearly impossible for some. Fear can be just as crippling as a disease or disability. 2 Timothy 1:7, ESV, says,

"For God has not given us a spirit of fear, but of power and of love and of sound mind."

3

You see, God didn't intend for us to have fear of any kind! Instead, He made us reliant on Him so that through Him, we can conquer every sin and fear that we encounter! When we are faced with fear, we can choose to let it cripple us or let it draw us closer to the Cross. There have been many times in my life when I have let fear cripple me, and I forget that God is my, "Light and Salvation." But the Lord reminds me that when I bring my fears to Him, He makes me more than a conqueror!

Day 3:
What is a Friend?

"A friend loves at all times, and a brother is born for a difficult time... One with many friends may be harmed, but there is a friend who stays closer than a brother."

Proverbs 17:17, 18:24 (ESV)

Do you ever find yourself questioning the relationships in your life? With your spouse? Your kids? Your parents? Your mentor? Even with your most intimate circle of friends? Maybe you're like me who's been damaged by false relationships, and you have a hard time recognizing the true ones. It can be so difficult to trust someone when you've been hurt deeply. Trust becomes hard to give. Being vulnerable becomes scary. Admitting that you need help becomes unthinkable. So, we allow the Enemy to tell us that we aren't worth being loved, and we just have to depend on ourselves and keep everything inside. But God tells us something totally different!

I continue to see the Lord's goodness and mercy in the midst of those hard moments. When it comes to someone who desires to serve others, one big reminder that God has given me is the gift and value of Godly friendship. I'm beyond thankful for the close friends in my life, especially for those who have become more like family to me! God has been recently teaching me the gift of community that I hadn't seen before. If you know me at all, then you know that I can be stubborn at times, and there are very personal reasons for that, and it's not easy to ask for help. Especially with learning to walk again, stubbornness increased! But, God has shown me that we can't do life on our own, we weren't created to! The "Friend" in this verse is actually referring to Jesus Himself!

One lesson in the Word is that when Jesus was in Gethsemane, hours before His death, He was in great distress, but He wasn't alone. He brought His three closest friends with Him in His suffering. I thought about that and said, "If Jesus needed His friends in the midst of suffering, then why do we think that we have to go through our suffering alone?" Now ultimately, God should be our biggest source of comfort, but He brings people into our lives to help and encourage us on the journey! I'm so thankful for the people He's brought into my life who point me to Christ, who choose to look past the physical limits, and who care about and love me unconditionally! Are you acquainted with Godly, close friends? But are you ultimately acquainted with the best Friend you could ever ask for? Don't wait, He is so excited to do life with you! What a Friend we have in Jesus!

Day 4:
No Sweeter Place to Be

"I'm so glad I learned to trust Him, Precious Jesus, Savior, Friend. And I know that He is with me, will be with me to the end."

Louisa M.R. Stead
Tis So Sweet to Trust in Jesus

I absolutely love the old hymn, "'Tis So Sweet to Trust in Jesus." This is a wonderful hymn that has always been a favorite of mine, as I have vivid memories of my Grandmother Annie humming this tune and others as she did her housework or worked outside. I can't think of a message that is more needed than what is conveyed in this hymn. The world around us is upside down (always has been), people are acting upon the natural sinful desires in our hearts (we always have). Even Believers can get caught up in the debates that our intention is to speak truth, yet we can often become engrossed with sharing, even that can lead to letting sinful pride lead, and completely miss the point of how God wants to use our influence. But this hymn was written by a missionary woman who was familiar with the chaos this world brings, the uncertainty of life, and endured great personal loss.

Yet, she knew that in the midst of her suffering, she learned how much she could fully count on Jesus. I've even seen the truths of this hymn seem to come more alive recently even during the most shattering moments, the frustration of thinking about letting go of certain goals and dreams, each pain filled day becomes more and more apparent, when the doctors tell me there is no cure. In the times of confusion that can overwhelm our thoughts and energy, I'm thankful for the wisdom of the Hymn Writers as they encourage us to hold tightly to the biblical truths we need today. With the chaos and uncertainties of this sinful world, we can be encouraged and encourage others that we can fully count on the Lord and how sweet it can be when we put our trust in Jesus.

Day 5:
Joy That Never Dies

"Joy doesn't come from our circumstances, it comes from our God."

Laura Story
When God Doesn't Fix It

Joy in Greek is, "Xapa`" meaning, rejoice. I told my dad that when I get a car, I want to have this as a bumper sticker or even my license plate! Joy is probably my favorite biblical term. Joy, to me, is when I read Scripture and discovering the treasures of God's character, and the promises He reminds me of. To me, joy is accomplishing a simple task that could take me moments or hours to do. To me, joy is sharing life with friends and students, just hearing what God's doing in their lives. To me, joy is knowing that I'm a sinner saved by the grace of God. God is faithful in giving a joy despite our circumstances, but He also gives us joy in the ordinary, the mundane, and in the middle of the chaos! Are you able to see the joy that the Lord wants to give you, and are you willing to share it with those around you, right where He has you? Joy enables us to relish in the hope and love that God gives, in whatever hard circumstances, stage of life, or just an ordinary day to day!

Jaclyn L. Young

Day 6:
Gratitude Leads to True Godliness

"Let the word of Christ dwell in you richly, teaching and admonishing one another in all wisdom, singing psalms, and hymns, and spiritual songs, with thankfulness in your hearts to God."

Colossians 3:16 (ESV)

On Thanksgiving Day, countless people will gather around the table with family, friends, and loved ones as we give thanks for God's blessings in our lives. Some tables will have an empty chair or two, other tables will be filled with the sounds of laughter, other tables will be filled with people but with sorrow and grief. Well, the more I thought about it, God brought to my thoughts to such a Thanksgiving table that was all of these at once. We often look at the Last Supper around Easter, but I believe it was truly the very first Thanksgiving...If you're old enough in the faith, you know the story well! Jesus asks the disciples to go and prepare the Passover for them. I imagine their dinner table looked like ours, filled with food and treats that weren't usually eaten. This was a celebration of remembrance for the Jewish People dating from Egypt, and beyond, of how God had delivered them from Egypt, and His unwavering covenant with them. They would sacrifice their spotless lamb as atonement and enjoy a feast. I imagine the disciples getting excited and wanting to make everything just perfect for Jesus. But I also imagine Jesus becoming solemn as He knows this is the last quality time with His friends, and He's probably trying to smile through it knowing it's only a matter of hours until His death.

Later on, everyone is laughing and joking around when Jesus kind of settles them down to start the meal. According to Matthew, Judas is already heading off to the chief priests to betray Jesus, and Jesus dismisses him, so everyone knows. Judas didn't just slip out. But Jesus carries on and gives thanks to the Father for the meal. Then, Jesus "took bread and after blessing it broke it and gave it to the disciples and said, 'Take, eat; this is my body.' And He took the cup, and when He had given thanks He gave it to them, saying, 'Drink of it, all of you, for this is my blood of the covenant, which is poured out for many for the forgiveness of sins. I tell you I will not drink again of this fruit of the vine until I drink it new within my Father's kingdom" (Matthew 26:26-29, ESV). So, this feast has gone from everyone having a good time, to an empty seat, and to sorrow. But, in verse 29, Jesus indicates that, yes, He's leaving Earth, but He's preparing an event bigger and better Thanksgiving feast! It will be at the Marriage Supper of the Lamb, where there will be great joy and laughter, there will be no empty seats, the table where the prodigal is welcomed, and there will be no sorrow. At that table, we will see Christ at the head, we will join hands, and give Him thanks and praise that in that moment, our faith has turned to sight. That is the Thanksgiving I am most anxious and excited for, are you?

Day 7:
What's So Great About Normal Anyway?

People with disabilities are the most normal in God's Economy."

Chad Smith

Joni and Friends Family Retreat

I was out shopping one day, and I was sitting down to take a break from the crazy, when this kid about 10 or 11 just stopped and took a good long stare at my brace and then kind of laughed at the sound of my voice. I just smiled and told him, "Hi." before he ran off. I couldn't help but think and pray, "Lord, I know everything is a blessing from You, even hardships. But sometimes I wonder what it'd be like if I were 'normal ' just for a short time." It was almost like I could hear God chuckle and reply, "If I had wanted you to be normal, I would have made you that way in the first place. I love you how I created you; yes, there are people who will scoff and laugh but I understand, and I will give you the strength to handle those situations with love and grace." I have these encounters with kids and even adults just about everywhere I go, but God has given me the most valuable tool to show others His glory and strength! I think the same scenario is true as Believers, we tend to want to blend in and be what society calls "normal," but doesn't Scripture tell us the opposite? We're called to stand out from the crowd despite what people say or think! God says, "As My child, you were not made to be normal. My Word says that they will laugh and scoff you because you belong to Me. But when you stay true to My Word and use the gifts I've given you, you will find your strength in Me."

Day 8:
When I Run, I Feel His Pleasure

"Have you not known? Have you not heard? The LORD is the Everlasting God. The Creator of the ends of the Earth. He does not grow weak or weary; His understanding is unsearchable. He gives power to the faint, and to him who has no might He increases strength. Even youths shall faint and be weary, and young men shall fall exhausted; but they who wait for the LORD shall renew their strength; they shall mount up with wings like eagles; they shall run and not be weary; they shall walk and not faint."

Isaiah 40:28-31 (ESV)

This passage has such a powerful influence in my life! The thought that we have an All-Knowing, All-Sufficient God Who provides us with the strength and endurance to face the challenges that come into our lives. To me, this passage offers so much encouragement and hope! Knowing that the Lord is always walking with us in our weaknesses, and that He doesn't leave us to fight on our own. Ever since I was a toddler, I've loved to run…I cannot tell you, friend, how many times I heard, "Jaclyn, don't run!" throughout my childhood! As a kid, I didn't understand why my body didn't allow me to do things that other kids were able to do. I so enjoyed trying to run and play with my sisters and cousins around our family farm, but I hated it when my body became too tired to keep up, and I ended up being left behind. Now, as an adult, I still deal with the same struggles as I did as a child. In high school, I could nearly run the distance of a 5K, and the goal was to complete an entire race by my senior year. Due to my most recent health decline, I have learned to walk all over again…sometimes it seems like taking one step forward then ten steps back. As my health deteriorates, so can my dreams of running. Often times, I will watch the film, Chariots of Fire, literally cheering on my sports hero, Eric Liddell. But, this passage reminds me that the one who trusts in God will be given His strength to keep fighting, and that One Day, I will run over mountains and valleys with no chronic pain, no fatigue, and no falling! Are you ready?

Day 9:
He Holds Purpose

"As Christians, we are not here for our own purpose at all-We are here for the purpose of God. And the two are not the same."

Oswald Chambers
My Upmost for His Highest

I've been pondering this question lately, "What is God's purpose for my life as a Believer?" "What is it that God has in mind for me?" These sound like very broad questions, and truthfully, they are. When I was a junior or senior in high school, I had been praying about the possibility of going overseas after college to work with people with disabilities who lived in very difficult countries. I had met with different pastors and missionaries who prayed with me and lead me in the Word as I took the beginning steps of this journey. I was actually invited to go to Kosovo and Nigeria by two different groups once I was well enough to travel. Of course, my family was hesitant but wanted to be supportive if this was what God wanted for me. In all honesty, my heart was no longer in the States, but elsewhere where people needed to hear the Gospel in unreached parts of the world. The hope and the plan was to get through six years of college, with degrees in Nonprofit Management and Missions. I was ready to hit the grind and get through college. I thought that this was my life's goal and purpose.

Though, God has a time for "every purpose under heaven." (Ecclesiastes 3:1) After an unexpected and unwanted decline in my health, I became frustrated because I felt like I had failed to live up to the calling that I was designed to fulfill. Being diagnosed with a chronic illness at the age of twenty-one was not part of the plan, and it has made it difficult to travel especially by air due to a lung condition as well. I remember lying in my rehab room unable to sleep, and I kept thinking and praying, "God, why would You put the passion and desire to go serve kids just like me who are treated so terribly and I'm here getting the best medical care in the world? It's just not fair!" I couldn't grasp the reality of how weak my body had become, and I didn't have a clue how He was going to use my current situation for the ministry that I wanted to build. I spent the next several months doing physical therapy and dealing with this frustration.

It wasn't until just before the holidays that I finally came to terms with that maybe God already has me where I'm meant to be, and where He needs me to make a difference. I am still seeing the unfolding of this, the gifts of building lifelong relationships, being able to serve more in my church and community, even the opportunity to write this book! God showed me that I didn't have to go very far to make a difference for His glory!

Day 10:
In His Arms, You Can Rest

"Come to Me, all who labor and are heavy laden, and I will give you rest. For My yoke is easy and my burden is light."
Matthew 11:28 (ESV)

The concept of this passage is, Jesus is indirectly reiterating the first Beatitude (Matthew 5:3) He is inviting the Jewish People who feel weighed down by the religious leaders and custom duties, to cast aside their attempts to be "good enough" or to even save themselves. As humans, we are stubborn and prideful, and we think that we can succeed in life on our own. But here, Jesus is saying something completely different. He wants us to stop trying to prove ourselves to Him and to others, and just rest in the knowledge that God will give us what we need for Spiritual growth and beyond.

Personally, this is probably the thing I struggle with the most. Due to having a physical disability, I have always strived to be as independent as possible. Sometimes, that independence can lead to stubbornness which ultimately leads to pride. When I'm trying to do something or accomplish a task that's just too hard for me to do, but I refuse someone's help, I'm saying to myself, "I don't need anyone!" when in reality we were made to be dependent on Someone. In order to be physically and emotionally replenished, we have to be spiritually replenished first and foremost!

"In a world that makes little sense, the Gospel is as simple as A,B,C."

"I would rather go through immense suffering in this life so I can long for the Joy in the Life to come."

"I think God allows difficult situations for us even as Believers, to examine where we find our security and our hope."

Day 11:
God's Outcomes are Better
than Our Suggestions

"For I know the plans I have for you,' declares the LORD,
'plans for welfare and not for evil, to give you a future and a hope."
Jeremiah 29:11 (ESV)

I'll never forget it! I was working my first retail job at LifeWay Christian Bookstore, and little boy about four or five years old, was following me around until I turned around and noticed him. He asked me, "What happened? What happened to you?" I smiled and replied, "It's just how God made me! I'll be ok!" The boy curiously smiled and ran back to his family. I thought about the encounter for the rest of the day. One must remember, this isn't an unusual interaction for me to have with children...some kids stare, laugh, imitate, even get scared and run away. But there are some who are curious and just want to know, "What happened?"

There was a time when I asked the Lord that question. As a ten-, and eleven-year-old, I learned how much my disability affected my life. I honestly went through a season of anger and grief. I asked God, "What happened? Why am I being punished? Why do people think I'm a freak? What did I do wrong?" Like the boy at work, I wondered, "What happened?" But, when God altered my view of my circumstances, and helped me understand the purpose of being different, I went from asking, "Why me?" to "Why NOT me?" It was through the Lord changing my perspective, that what happened to me physically didn't matter, it's what happened to me spiritually was what mattered! I discovered that the physical limits have no hindrance on what God can do in and through me! I wouldn't be honest if I said that there aren't days when I wish I didn't have CP... To be truthful, I can often wonder what it might have been like to have a "normal" life. However, it's been through those painful and exhausting times and my journey with CP, where I've seen the Lord work and strengthen my faith and trust in Him. We may never know why certain things happen in our lives, but when we view them as a means to walk alongside others who are suffering, and to grow in our dependence and trust in Christ, then, "Why NOT me?"

Day 12:
What God Ordains is Always Good

"Shout for joy, you heavens! Earth, rejoice! Mountains break into joyful shouts! For the LORD has comforted his people and will have compassion on his afflicted ones."

Isaiah 49:13 (ESV)

One of the highlights of my week is being able to go to choir practice every Wednesday night at my church! Even though I don't sing on stage, nothing brings me more excitement and joy than to worship the Lord, build friendships, and getting the inside scoop on the amazing music!

One of my favorite songs that the choir sings, is about what God ordains is always good and it really hits home for me in many personal ways. Every night at choir practice, we'd sing this song and every time, tears would form in my eyes... even this morning! I was reminded of how we often forget to see God's goodness and don't see the joy that suffering can bring.

As I listened to the choir sing, the Lord brought to mind that through the suffering, we are to submit to Him, and He wants us to realize that we ultimately need Him and we don't have to go through it on our own. Sometimes, we let the trials "cripple" us, or we can ask God, "Why me?" But, if we stop and remember that Scripture says that God doesn't put us in difficult situations to harm us, but to help us grow and see our need for Him. We may never know or understand why we have to endure the suffering that we have to go through, but God promises us that what He ordains is always good.

Day 13:
When We Fall, He Doesn't Leave Us There

"No amount of falls will really undo us. If we keep picking ourselves up each time...it is when we notice the dirt that God is most present in us; it is the very sign of His presence."

C.S. Lewis
(Quote from letter to Mary Neylen. 1942)

Having CP, I fall all the time...As a child, I would fall and most times I'd fall and have a bloody knee or bruised up elbow. Sometimes, I got up crying and frustrated that I couldn't keep up with the other kids. But most of the time, I stood up, regrouped, and got right back into the action! But, each time I fell, I had a choice to make...I could stay down and put limitations on myself. However, I could fall, stand up, and allow it to help me grow and not let it keep me from doing what I wanted to do. The same thing is true in undergoing trials. When we fall, and experience hardships of various types, do we allow them to limit our dependence on Christ and our spiritual growth, or do we look at our trials as a means to deepen our love for God and to see His faithfulness on a whole new level? I know it broke my parent's hearts to watch me fall over and over again, but they held back and allowed it because they knew that was the only way I would learn to get back up on my own, and gain independence.

In the same way, it breaks God's heart to see us suffering, but He wants the trial or the "fall" to draw us back to Him. As I spend the next several months recovering from surgery, I can often feel like I'm a little kid who has to have help with everything, and I ask God why I had to go through this right now, why can't I do the things other "normal" twenty-five-year-olds are doing. I can feel like that little girl left behind by the other kids. Falling is in the nature of the Believer's life, just like it's in the nature of a patient with CP. But the choice remains the same. We have to choose to stay down or get back up. When I fall physically or spiritually, God gently reminds me, "Jaclyn, it hurts Me to watch you fall and struggle every moment of the day. I know you wish sometimes Cerebral Palsy didn't exist, and it could be cured, but I'm allowing it because I'm using it as a platform for My glory. When you fall, I seem far away, but I have never been closer. It's time to get back up, don't give up!"

Day 14:
The Lord Remembers His Beloved

"Pass me not, O gentle Savior; hear my humble cry. While on others Thou art calling, do not pass me by."

Fanny Crosby
Pass Me Not, O Gentle Savior

This has become one of my favorite hymns. I love how it illustrates a picture of how sometimes in times of trial and frustration, we tend to believe that God is distant or has overlooked our plea for rescue. Do you feel that way in your own trials? I know I do. Personally, it's during times of loneliness and isolation that I get discouraged. When it's hard to be able to jump in the car when my friends head out on the weekends, watching friends go abroad or start dating, even being sick and having to stay "secluded" for a while. It's in these moments when I can feel left out or passed by. I can find myself second guessing things, is my disability a blessing when it seems like a hinderance? Do others really see evidence of Christ in my life?

These questions reel through my mind and there are times when I almost believe the lies that the Enemy wants me to believe. However, the last stanza of the hymn says, "Thou the stream of all my comfort; more than life to me. Whom have I on earth beside Thee? Whom in heaven but Thee? Savior, Savior, hear my humble cry! While on others Thou art calling, do not pass me by." This brings much comfort to me! Though it seems that God is far from our reach, it's in those times when He's closest to us. He doesn't overlook our sorrows, tune out our cries, pass by our pain. Quite the contrary! The Lord is our greatest Comfort, and all of our joy can be found in Him. When I get lonely or frustrated, there is no greater comfort that Christ is holding me close, that He's a Friend to lean upon, and He's a gentle savior who doesn't pass me by!

Day 15:
What Could Be Better?

"Better is a little with the fear of the LORD than great treasure and trouble with it. Better is a dinner of herbs where love is than a fattened ox and hatred with it."

Proverbs 15:16-17 (ESV)

Every summer, I like to try and pick a book of the Bible that I know little or nothing about. So, I began reading Proverbs for my summer study. I think we often just pull out the more well-known chapters and verses, and we overlook the ones in between that can have so many riches packed into them. I was shown such verses only yesterday. If you're not very familiar with the book of Proverbs, King Solomon of Israel wrote this calling for Jews and later on, first century Christians to seek Godly wisdom in every area of their life. Solomon spends the first few chapters basically saying, "There is nothing more important or crucial in a person's heart than heeding Godly wisdom." He says wisdom is far more valuable than all the riches of the world. I find it kind of ironic than the wealthiest king in history makes this statement. Beyond that, Solomon also wrote Ecclesiastes, where he pretty much spends the entire book saying that life apart from God is meaningless and worthless. So, with that bit of a long introduction, here's my point: The point Solomon is making in these verses, is that it's better to lack worldly possessions and have Godly wisdom, than to have riches and not experience the love of God. I think if Solomon could pick a generation of people to repeat this to, this would be it.

I also thought of a rather strange but accurate picture of this. In his novel, A Christmas Carol, Charles Dickens displays how

Scrooge had all the money and possessions he could ask for, but he didn't share his gifts, his time, or his heart with those around him leaving him cold and bitter. On the other hand, the Cratchit family who had very little in the way of money, resources, rare pleasures, and not to mention a dying son. Surely, they would be miserable. But the Cratchit family, knowing what little they had materially, they still gathered around the dinner table joyful and thankful for what they did have, and they relished in the love they had for each other. Likewise, we as Believers should relish in the wisdom and love of God as Solomon instructs. I can often forget this truth and say to God, "I wish I had that ability, and not this disability. I wish I could run more and fall less...etc." But the Lord shows me that what I lack physically, I gain spiritually by seeking His wisdom, and growing in my relationship with Him! Even when we lack in what the world says is pleasurable, and fulfilling, it has no equivalent to what we gain in Christ.

Day 16:
The Two Greatest Words to Hear

"His master said to him, 'Well done, good and faithful servant.
You have been faithful over a little; I will set you over much. Enter
the joy of your master."

Matthew 25:21 (ESV)

In this passage, we heard from Jesus about how to be truly ready for His future coming and reign on earth. As Believers, we should always be in anticipation for Christ's return. However, in the parable of the talents, Jesus makes it clear that God gives each of us unique gifts and talents in order to advance His gospel and glorify God with them. We are not meant to receive the gift of salvation then keep it to ourselves. God doesn't give us our spiritual gifts only for us to bury them as the third servant had done. We are to multiply the bounty that God has laid out and invite others to join in the Feast of eternal life and satisfaction!

Luke 12:48b says, "Everyone to whom much was given, of him much will be required, and from him to whom they entrusted much, they will demand the more." God chooses to give and entrust us with many gifts, because He desires us to turn around and lay them at His feet to do with as He pleases. I know that I've recently discovered that one of my spiritual gifts, though it may not seem like much to some, but making myself available to friends of all ages and walks of life, and to love on them and just give them a friend to talk to and spend time with them. What do you think some of your gifts and talents are, and how are you using them to advance the kingdom of God as well as anticipating Christ's return? Are you prepared for Christ to look upon you and say, "Well done, good and faithful servant" (Matthew 25:21, ESV).

Day 17:
God is Strong Enough to Carry You

"God is our refuge and strength, a helper who is always found in times of trouble...He says, 'Be still, and know that I am God; I will be exalted among the nations, I will be exalted in the earth."

Psalms 46:1,10 (ESV)

God is strong enough; I don't have to act tough all the time. It's okay to admit I'm hurting; the Lord is my greatest Comfort. Because of Christ, I'm worthy to be loved and cared for, now I'm called to love and care for others in the same manner. There are moments when it can be hard to, "be still." When we get restless, the last thing we want to do is to be still and wait for God's timing. Personally, it's hard for me to be still during times of impatience, whether it's something as simple as jumping ahead to get my full license and have the freedom to go wherever I want, whenever I want! But this passage talks about a concept of "being still" that goes far beyond our mundane situations like driving. This is talking about a stillness in the midst of our brokenness. A stillness where the Lord leads us so we can hear His voice.

Sometimes, I think this is a stillness we don't often ask or hope for, we don't like going through trials...But that's where God can speak to us the most, and we have to be obedient and chose to listen to what He wants us to learn. I know that in my personal struggles, I can become restless, when I'm in pain, when there's so much uncertainty around me, even when the Enemy likes to creep in and tell me lies that he wants me to believe. It's in those moments when it's hardest to be still and listen for my Father's voice. It's difficult to stop and allow God to speak truth into our hearts. Yet, He's always speaking to us in the trials and brokenness, telling us that we have the assurance that the trial is for our good, that He's with us in the midbar...we can just "Be still and know that He is God."

Day 18:
A Place to Belong

"God has a special place for those who feel left out."

Max Lucado

My favorite Christmas story to read as a child was The Crippled Lamb. It tells the story of a lamb named Joshua, who was born with a leg that didn't form correctly. Josh didn't like being different. He felt sad when he saw the other sheep with all white wool, since he had black spots with black feet, he felt lonely when he saw the other lambs with their moms and dads since he had neither a mom nor a dad. But Josh felt saddest when he had to watch the other lambs run and play since he couldn't with his crippled leg. Joshua didn't understand why God allowed him to be born with a disability. The other lambs laughed at him and left him behind as he struggled to keep up with the flock. I think I know how Josh felt.

With the slow and gradual deterioration of my strength, the decrease in my energy, the pain the comes with breathing, and it seems my hard days outnumber my better days...sometimes, I can feel left behind and out of place like Josh did. The frustration became real one night close to Christmas. During those few moments of just deep sadness and fear of almost giving up, God reminded me of the end of Josh's story. The Shepard had left Josh behind in fear that he wouldn't make it to the next valley. Never before had Josh felt so sad and left out...Josh's friend Abigail would tell him, "Don't be sad little Joshua, God has a special place for those who feel left out." How true! At the end of the story, Josh understood why he'd been born with a crippled leg. Since he was different, he wasn't in the valley with the other sheep, instead he was among the first to welcome Jesus into the world! This was a reminder I desperately needed tonight. I don't know if I'll fully recover, I don't know what it would be like without the struggle and pain that CP brings; truthfully, I don't want to know! However, I know one thing for sure, God has a special purpose for all the gifts He gives, including a disability. Friend, whenever you start wondering where you belong, one thing is certain. There is no better place to be than in the arms of the Good Shepherd.

Day 19:
God Will Use Great Trials for Great Victories

"There is no more devastating blow against evil then when a human being chooses God in the face of suffering, disappointment, unbelief, chronic pain, frustration, abandonment...before the circumstances change, to get up and proclaim that God is good, is a devastating blow to evil."

John Eldredge

Do you have days where you wish your trial was just a dream, and you all you had to do was shoot up out of bed for it to be over? But, in that endless "dream," the Lord sends you the words you need to hear. During times of frustration and pain, my prayer is that I don't allow the Enemy to use the circumstances to hinder my reliance on Christ. It can be so easy to do. But I also pray that I allow God to use the circumstances to shape me to become more and more like Him and that it's evident to others that I trust in Him for my sole strength. When the frustration comes, in the moment, I wish I could be freed from pain, that I could walk easier, or that I could change just one part of the CP. But Satan likes to try to turn the frustration into discontent and even bitterness.

Job is a great example of this, God allowed Satan to take everything away from Job. Yet, Job remained faithful and steadfast through each trial he went through. Nothing makes Satan cringe more than when we go through hardships and remain strong in our walk with God. The Bible is filled with passages that help us defeat Satan's lies and schemes. There is no other way. It's through our

37

dependence and trust in the Lord that we can walk through suffering triumphantly and allow Him to grow us and we will become who He designed us to be. To become more like Christ is the ultimate goal of suffering and trust me, I would much rather go through the pain of having a disability if I get to lean on Jesus every step of the way!

Day 20:
He Only Gives the Best

"Every good gift and every perfect gift is from above, coming down from the Father of lights, with whom there is no variation or shadow due to change. Of His own will He brought us forth by the word of truth, that we should be a kind of first fruits of His creatures."

James 1:17-18 (ESV)

There's a country song called, "Unanswered Prayers." The chorus goes like this, "Sometimes I thank God for unanswered prayers. Remember when you're talking to the Man upstairs. Just because He doesn't answer, doesn't mean He don't care. Some of God's greatest gifts are unanswered prayers." Though this song means to provide comfort to suffering people, it's not right theology! The firm Believer knows that God always answers prayer...sometimes He says, "yes" other times He says, "no." But He still answers! Can you look back and remember those painful moments that God said, "no" and you see it as one of the greatest gifts He could give you? Maybe, your husband got laid off from a well-paying job, and he ended up working at a local grocery store. You watch your child suffer from an illness that will eventually lead them to die. Maybe you're the couple who planned, hoped, and prayed for a house full of children, and the doctor told you that you cannot conceive. Or maybe you're the child who has spent years or even decades praying for your ailing parent to come to Christ, but it ends up being too late.

How do you wrap your mind around those heartbreaking situations, and you find yourself almost believing that God isn't really listening? You tell God that if He gave you that one desire, you would never ask Him for anything again. This is how many people, including Believers, approach prayer. I know I have thought this way. We think that only the good things in life are beneficial, so we ask God to let us skip the bad things. In the verse above, James has been telling us before that our trials serve a purpose and leads us to an Eternal Reward. Throughout the entire Bible, we discover so many people who received God's abundant blessings, but He took them through intense suffering so they could experience the full value of the outcome. No, not every prayer was answered in the way they wanted, but each one knew and trusted that the Lord had their best interests at heart! Friend, it's normal to be frustrated when God doesn't answer our prayers in our time. But it should bring us relief and comfort knowing that He always answers in a way that will draw us closer to Him.

Day 21:
It's Not About Us

"Suffering is my gain; I bow to my Heavenly Father's will, and receive it hushed and still; suffering is my worship now."

Jean Paul

I believe that the ultimate purpose of our difficulties and trials is to glorify God. Scripture says that there's a reason for each trial that we endure, and the goal as Believers is to honor and glorify God in every area of our lives, and that includes suffering. This doesn't mean that God wants us to suffer, He doesn't take pleasure in watching us go through hardships, but He knows that the trial is going to shape us into becoming more like Him, it refines us and draws us closer to Him, and so that we can bring Him glory. But, worshipping God in suffering is a choice, right? I have to wake up every day and decide, am I going to allow my disability or chronic pain stop me from doing what God has given me to do today? Or am I going to praise the Lord and look for the blessings?

Perhaps you have gone through or are in the midst of a trial where you find it difficult to praise God. Truthfully, we can find it easier to hold onto the pain and difficulties. However, when we come to understand that God is with us in the trials and that He ordains them, then there is a joy and a satisfaction we can have! God is worthy of our worship, even in suffering. Through times of deep pain and sorrow, I have seen the Lord grow my faith in more ways than I could have ever imagined! When our sufferings deepen, our love and hope in Christ grows far deeper. No one asks for hardships, but if they bring us to a deeper level of worship, then that is worth every trial and every tear! You know, I think it's kind of special that

God has entrusted me with this suffering so that I can worship Him in a way that I never thought I could!

Day 22:
What Are You Here For?

"Look carefully then how you walk, not as unwise but as wise, making the best use of the time, because the days are evil. Therefore, do not be foolish, but understand what the will of the Lord is."

Ephesians 5:15-17 (ESV)

As with most writers, I can go through times where I can ask questions like, "Is my perspective on my circumstances right with what Scripture teaches? Do I live out what I speak and write about? Can anyone learn anything from my perspective? Am I taking the time to learn from other people's perspectives and life experiences?" Everyone's perspective comes from the different circumstances and challenges they go through in life. A perspective also allows us to connect and teach others about how we view and handle whatever happens in life. For me, my perspective, or my point of view, has come through the lens of a disability. CP has allowed me to not only to view the world differently, but has taught me that God looks at the heart, as should I.

Also, it's been through this perspective that God has shown me a deeper level of Who He is, and who I am in Christ. However, that's only part of where my perspective comes from. As Christians, we are to look at the world through the eyes of Christ. When we see others go through hard circumstances, or ourselves, we are meant to view them as Jesus does. We see all throughout Scripture, that in Jewish culture, people with disabilities or who were at the bottom of the social ladder, people didn't want much to do with them. Their perspective was not compassion, maybe God was punishing them for sin, they saw no potential. But Jesus came to change that! He took what people saw as feeble and made it strong. He took what people saw as weak and made it mighty. He took what people saw as a disability and made it into a blessing. This is how Jesus wanted His disciples to gain this perspective, and He wants us to gain it as well. The best part of having a Christ-like perspective, is the eternal perspective we gain. We can look at our trials and circumstances as only a speck on the timeline of Eternity. When we have a Christ-like and an eternal perspective, we will not view life the same way again!

Day 23:
Do We Even Matter?

"And even the very hairs of your head are all numbered. So, don't be afraid; you are worth more than many sparrows. Whoever acknowledges me before others, I will also acknowledge before my Father in heaven."

Matthew 10:30-32 (ESV)

Do you ever question how you fit into God's plan? You doubt that you have much to offer, and wonder if who you are is enough? I think everyone does at some point! Thinking through thoughts of questioning, and trying to figure out what God says, my mind went back to a book I read as a child. Just the Way You Are tells the story of five orphans who were about to be adopted by the king. Full of excitement, the children began to wonder how different their lives were going to be! The villagers told them that they needed to present gifts to win the approval of the king. They said, "Only those with great gifts are worthy to live with the king!"

Long story short, all the children, except one, started to prepare their gifts. The youngest sister firmly believed she had no gift. She wasn't an artist or musician, she spent her time at the city gates caring for animals, she knew the beggars by name, she would ask questions and be anxious to hear of people's life stories. Her only gift was her heart, but she didn't recognize it. At the end, while the other children were too busy, they missed the king's arrival, but the girl made time for the king, gave him the gift of her time, her care, her love.

I guess, sometimes I feel like the girl who thought she had no gift, that I can't go on international mission trips, or do physically demanding projects, so I can think that I don't have much to offer. But I've come to realize that God gives us all gifts. For some, it's music, art, showing hospitality, serving in different ministries. Our worth isn't in what we do, it's found in who we are in Christ! I can get frustrated when I want to try things but can't physically do so. For one, I see how God's gifted me with the time to work, write, invest and spend time with those who may need a friend, and He's called me to glorify Him with the gifts He has given me and what I can do. God doesn't need us to prove anything to Him, He only asks us to come as we are, and that we are to view our gifts as invaluable ways to share the freedom, love, and the joy we have in Christ!

Day 24:
Fear Has No Hold

"Humble yourselves, therefore, under the mighty hand of God so that at the proper time He may exalt you, casting all your anxieties on Him, because He cares for you. Be sober-minded; be watchful. Your adversary the devil prowls around like a roaring lion, seeking someone to devour. Resist him, firm in your faith, knowing that the same kinds of suffering are being experienced by your brotherhood throughout the world."

1 Peter 5:6-9 (ESV)

A favorite song of mine is called, "Fear is a Liar." To be honest, I probably listen to this song multiple times a day, I make my dad blare the radio every time it comes on in the car (even louder when I'm driving, so I can block out his inaccurate accusations against my wonderful driving!) But this song has just become an anthem that God has used to remind me of the Truth. We live in a world today that's pretty engulfed in fear, fear of war, fear of natural disaster, fear of famine and disease, fear of what's different…these are more global fears. On a more personal level, we fear things like, death, uncertainty, loss, illness, just to name a few.

So, what is it that you fear? I know that I struggle with many fears…for instance with my hip surgery being only a month away, I fear that the surgery won't do its job, fear that my recovery will take longer or that I won't recover as well as expected, fear that I'll spend large amounts of time alone in the hospital or the rehab center, or even the fear of being a burden and an inconvenience to those around me. These and others are real fears that I struggle with almost daily. However, what is fear? Or a better question, WHO is

Fear? If you read the chorus of this song, it says, "Fear, HE is a liar." It doesn't say, "Fear, IT is a liar" but, "HE is a liar." Fear is a living Being, Fear has a voice we can actually hear, Fear has feet that walk swiftly to deceive, Fear has a name, Satan.

Since the Beginning, Satan has sought to instill fear, doubt, and lies in our minds and hearts. John 8:44 tells us, "You are of your father the devil, and your will is to do your father's desires. He was a murderer from the beginning, and does not stand in the truth, because there is no truth in him. When he lies, he speaks out of his own character, for he is a liar and the father of lies." Jesus is telling us here that it is in Satan's nature to lie and bring fear into our hearts. So, when he tells me, "Jaclyn, you aren't strong enough, your disability is a crutch, you're not truly wanted or loved, you will always be weak and incapable of greatness." It's in his nature to tell me those lies. In contrast, Truth wins out fear! Again, in John 14:6, Jesus declares, "I am the way, truth, and the life. No one comes to the Father except through Me." Scripture doesn't say that Jesus knows Truth, or that He acknowledges Truth, but that He IS Truth itself. To close out, if God is Truth and that He gives us that Truth in written Scripture, then we have the most powerful Tool to fight against Satan's lies and when we are in Christ, there is no room for fear!

Day 25:
The Ultimate Duty

"So, Jesus said to them, 'Truly, truly, I say to you, the Son can do nothing of His own accord, but only what He sees the Father doing. For whatever the Father does, that the Son does likewise. For the Father loves the Son and shows Him all that He Himself is doing. And greater works than these will he show him, so that you may marvel. For as the Father raises the dead and gives them life, so also the Son gives life to whom he will. For the Father judges no one, but has given all judgment to the Son, that all may honor the Son, just as they honor the Father. Whoever does not honor the Son does not honor the Father who sent Him. Truly, truly, I say to you, whoever hears my word and believes Him who sent me has eternal life. He does not come into judgment but has passed from death to life."

John 5:19-24 (ESV)

During one of my writer's block moments, and I asked the Lord to truly remind me of what my calling actually is and how to live it out according to Scripture. As always, God answered my earnest request, and showed me in my brief period of doubt, what I'm called to as a Believer which led me to write down these five points that helped me to fully understand what I'm called to as a speaker, a writer, a friend, and as a servant of the Lord.

1. I am called to accept salvation, I was predestined to be one of God's Elect, He chose me to be a part of His Family. (Romans 8:29)

2. I am called to grow and become more like Him, God desires for me to get to know Him and enjoy spending time with Him. To want

and crave to be in His presence. (Psalms 119)

3. I am called to love others, if I say that I love God, but I don't love my neighbor or even my enemy, then I bear a false testimony. But, if I love them, then there is evidence of the Gospel within me. (Matthew 5:43-48)

4. I am called to praise God in my suffering, the trials that God allows, are just hurdles on the racetrack of life. God doesn't allow them too high or throws them out there at random, He strategically places them where we need the most spiritual growth. He knows that we have the strength in Him to overcome each of them. (Philippians 3:14)

5. I am called to proclaim the Gospel in whatever capacity God chooses. Whether it's on the stage, at my job, in my home, in my church, and even in the hospital room. (1 Corinthians 1:26-31)

This is my Calling as a Christian, to serve God in every circumstance, trial, uncertainty, fear, and triumph. I was made to bring glory to God! Have you answered the Call as a Believer in your own life?

Day 26:
He Doesn't Make Mistakes

"I praise you for I am fearfully and wonderfully made. Wonderful are your works; my soul knows it very well."

Psalms 139:14 (ESV)

I read through Psalm 139 for my quiet time one year on my birthday. I've read this passage many times before but it kind of took on a different meaning for me that particular day. When it says, "My frame was not hidden from you, when I was being made in secret, intricately woven in the depths of the earth." We can easily rephrase that by saying He "crafted" us and was so detailed in how He fashioned us into who we are. It's like how a wood carver carefully carves each part of the artwork, he doesn't rush, he makes sure that the project will function properly and fulfill the purpose he has for it to accomplish. This is what God does with us! I realized that when God crafted me, He didn't rush, or make a mistake. He strategically crafted me exactly how I would fulfill my purpose for His glory.

Growing up, close family and friends would talk about the night I was born. My favorite part of the account was after the first critical hours, the doctor came and told my parents that there really wasn't a medical reason I survived. My dad replied, "There are people all over the world praying for this baby. We know Who spared her, He has something big for her!" The doctor who claimed to be an atheist, wrote in my chart, "miraculous turn around." Years later, I've seen God's goodness, it's only by His grace that I'm here. I'm nothing special, I just want to do what God asks of me. I am thankful for my physical health, but I am so much more thankful for my Spiritual healing through the truth of the Gospel! Somedays, I don't understand why God chose this path for me. I tend to wonder, "There are many others who can probably speak better, can be a better influence, they have more resources than I do. I'm not really good for ministry."

Then I remember that this way is demeaning to God. When we dive into self-condemnation, we are telling God that He created something flawed. But we see that the Bible teaches the contrary. Yet, once we accept the path that God has laid out for us, and commit to following in faithfulness, we will discover how involved God is in our lives. Friend, you are not a mistake! Take heed to the truth that the Lord knows exactly who you are, and who He has created you to be. He cares for you and reminds you that you are so wonderfully made.

Day 27:
Grace, Unending Grace!

"For by grace you have been saved through faith. And this is not your own doing; it is the gift of God, not a result of works, so that no one may boast."

Ephesians 2:8-9 (ESV)

What is the greatest gift you've ever received? I was extremely close to my Great-Grandmother. When she passed away, she left me one of her most valuable possessions. There was nothing more precious and meaningful to me than Grandmother leaving me such a priceless gift. It told me that she deeply cherished our close relationship, and that of all the other grandchildren, she wanted me to have it. Sadly, that heirloom came up missing, and was never recovered until later. I often feel unworthy to have been entrusted with such a gift that couldn't be replaced. I think the same concept can relate to our salvation...Grace means, "the free and unmerited favor of God, as manifested in the salvation of sinners and the bestowal of blessings." There is nothing we can do to earn God's grace. Because of our sin nature, we think we have to earn grace and Eternity, we think we have to be smart enough, strong enough, and good enough to earn grace. The World's mentality is that nothing is free and there's always a cost or a catch.

People skeptical of the Gospel will sometimes ask, "What's the catch? It's just too good to be true." However, Christ offers us salvation freely, no strings attached! When Jesus satisfied the wrath of God, He paid the ultimate price so salvation can indeed be free. When someone gives you a gift you don't ask how much it costs or reject it. You take it graciously. So, God offers us grace as a gift, the price is paid in full, and by faith we can have assurance of our favor in God's eyes. Just as I didn't ask for or do anything to deserve my Grandmother's gift, she offered it to me out of her love for me. As so, God chose us for salvation, not by our own works, but because He is a loving and gracious Father, who calls us to Himself just as we are!

Day 28:
He Holds Us by the Strength of His Hand

*"Three times I pleaded with the Lord about this, that it should
leave me. But he said to me, 'My grace is sufficient for you, for my
power is made perfect in weakness.' Therefore, I will boast all the
more gladly of my weaknesses, so that the power of Christ may rest
upon me. For the sake of Christ, then, I am content with weaknesses,
insults, hardships, persecutions, and calamities. For when I am
weak, then I am strong."*

2 Corinthians 12:8-10 (ESV)

My absolute favorite passage in all of Scripture is 2 Corinthians
12:1-10. If you are unfamiliar with this passage, the apostle Paul is
struggling with a "thorn in the flesh..." We could almost translate
this phrase in modern terms and say that Paul had some type of
"disability." Recent theologians believe that it was more than likely
an emotional and psychological state than a physical ailment.
Although, we're never told what his disability was, but we do know
that he begged and pleaded with God to take it away and heal him.
But God's reply in verse 9 gave Paul the confidence and strength he
needed to withstand the trial. I often turn to this passage when I find
myself ready to throw in the towel and give up.

The following poem was written on a day where I found myself
in bed unable to move, and God in His faithfulness brought these
words and phrases together when I needed them most. When our
trials become overwhelming, God wants to lead us into the stillness
of His peace to remind us that He is in total control, and His grace
is sufficient! My worship pastor asked some time ago if I would

be willing to compose a poem based on this passage that could be transformed into a choir piece. (When he has writer's block, he will sometimes enlist my help, so we can't have writer's block at the same time!) But, in the middle of a pain filled night, the Lord was very timely in weaving the piece below together.

I feel too broken to mend, I don't seem to understand. I'm tired and weary; O Lord where is Your hand? Foes are mighty, and waves are strong; how can I make it to the end? Why, Father, does the pain have to last so long?

And He said to me, "My grace is sufficient for you. Dear Child, I know the road is tough and the way seems unclear; I'm here, and I'll give you the strength to withstand the test and lead you into your Eternal Rest. I will dry your tears, so have no fear; for your God will carry you through, My grace is sufficient for you."

Well, the night may seem so dark, and the fight can look too hard; but take heart, He's been with you from the start. The Lord will shelter you, He understands your pain, and He hears your cry. Just hold on, for He has never left your side.

He gently whispers, "My grace is sufficient for you. Dear Child, I know the road is tough and the way seems unclear; I'm here, and I'll give you the strength to withstand the test and lead you into your Eternal Rest. I will dry your tears, so have no fear; for your God will carry you through, My grace is sufficient for you."

Day 29:
Total Surrender

"Whatever you do, work at it with all your heart as working for the Lord not for men."

Colossians 3:23 (ESV)

Throughout my young teenage years, into the early years of college, I have seen people who are saved but walked away from God because they were pursuing their relationship with Him. They thought God should serve them and are waiting to be served. What does it mean to be totally surrendered? First, we must learn what "surrendered" means:

Surrender- to give up; to abandon.

To be surrendered to Christ means we have to abandon ourselves of our flesh and tell God He is totally in control of our lives.

What does a surrendered life look like? Once you lay everything before God you want to start your new walk with accountability partners, daily Bible reading, get involved at church. Now, I'm not saying do things for attention or credit, do it for Jesus.

Another way to live a surrendered life is to share God's love with others. God gives a joy and a satisfaction in our relationship, but He didn't give it to us to keep. He gave it to us to take to the ends of the earth. That was a command from Jesus!

As I go through current trials, I can't stop smiling and thinking how good and gracious God is! I wasn't supposed to walk or talk, or even live, but our great and powerful Lord had something big in mind for me. I don't regret surrendering to Christ, He showed me my purpose in life. And it's satisfying. So, what about you? Are you ready for a lifetime experience? It's going to be hard, but you won't regret it.

Day 30:
All Creatures, Praise His Name!

My pastor once went through a sermon series about how God reveals Himself through Creation, and I was convicted of how I forget how detailed God is, and how involved He is in our lives. Please accept my deepest apologies for the length of this, but between the Lord's direction and my nature as a writer, it was very difficult to put my "pen" down! As I've learned and studied, I started to jot down words and phrases from several passages of Scripture, and just being in awe of Who God is, this piece was written.

Before there was time, He was eternal.
Before a living being roamed the Earth, He was Triune
Before angels fell before Him, He was worshipped
Who is this big and independent Creator?
He is God.

After Adam sinned, He sought to rescue
After Moses doubted, He gave strength
After David fled, He was a refuge
After Job lost everything, He sustained
After Israel turned away, He pursued
Who is this One Who seeks, saves, and redeems?
He is God.

When Mary was frightened, He assured
When the angels sang, He was praised
When the disciples followed, He guided
When the crowds gathered, He taught
Who is this Man that heals, brings life, and salvation?
He is God.

While he twelve broke bread, He was setting the example
While His friends slept, He prayed, "Let this pass from Me."
While He was being tried and convicted, He kept silent
While He was on the Cross, He was accomplishing the Mission
While He took His last breath, He vanquished every sin
Who is this righteous Lamb Who bestows forgiveness and
grace?
He is God.

As the stone rolled away, He breathed again
As He exited the grave, He conquered death
As the women ran from the empty tomb, He proclaimed victory
As they witnessed His ascension, He commanded them to,
"Go."
Who is this triumphant King Who now lives again?
He is God.

Now, as we go through trials, He provides comfort
Now, as we obey His Word, He promises blessing
Now, as we share the Good News, He saves whoever calls on
His name
Now, as we wait, serve, and hope, He shall indeed return
Who is this One Who chose, loves, and makes sinners His
Bride?
He is God.

AFTERWORD

Insights from the Curb is a collection of journal entries that Jaclyn has written over the course of her teenage and young adult years. Jaclyn accepted Christ as her Savior at the age of eight and has clung to the truth and hope of the Gospel since. As a child with Cerebral Palsy, Jaclyn could not always participate in many activities that most children enjoy. Though not being able to do certain activities, this gave Jaclyn ample opportunity to begin to know and study God's Word at an early age. As she grew firm in her faith, Jaclyn realized that maybe God had a very unique purpose for the unique path He had chosen for her. In her teen years, Jaclyn began journaling, and writing commentary-style entries for many church newsletters, and then sharing them on social media. Jaclyn has also shared her story and journey of faith with various youth groups, schools, and benefit events. Jaclyn always desires for her readers and listeners to know the Biblical and theological context of Scripture, as, "no mere man can add to the Word of God." She states. It was through her love for Scripture and knack for writing, Insights from the Curb was written. Today, Jaclyn is thankful that she had to miss out on much as a child, so she could truly learn how to walk in obedience to what God has called her to do. Jaclyn's prayer is that all those who read her work will be encouraged by her observations and be challenged to grow deeper in their own walk with Christ or begin the journey of a lifetime with Him.

BIBLIOGRAPHY

All Scripture quotations are taken from The Holy Bible, the English Standard Version, copyright 2013, 2018 by Crossway. All rights reserved.

"Tis So Sweet to Trust in Jesus." South Africa. Louisa M.R. Stead. 1882.

Story, Laura. *When God Doesn't Fix It.* (W. Publishing Group, An Imprint of Thomas Nelson, 2015).

Smith, Chad. *"People with Disabilities Are Normal."* (Flat Rock, North Carolina. August 2016).

Chambers, Oswald. *"My Upmost for His Highest."* (Dodd, Mead & Co. New York. 1935).

Lewis, C.S. *"From a letter to Mary Neylen."* (January 20, 1942).

"Pass Me Not, O Gentle Savior." United States. Fanny J. Crosby. 1868. of Burning Words of Brilliant Writers (1895).

Lucado, Max. *"The Crippled Lamb."* (Word Publishing, 1994).

Paul, Jean. *"Dictionary of Burning Words of Brilliant Writers."* P. 568. (1895).

John Eldredge quote, citation unknown.

ABOUT THE AUTHOR

JACLYN YOUNG, an advocate for people with special needs, knows from firsthand experience about living life with a disability. Diagnosed with cerebral palsy as an infant, Jaclyn knows both the challenges and blessings a disability can bring. Jaclyn has brought awareness to the special needs population through motivational speaking and writing. In her first book, a devotional, Jaclyn shares struggles and joys she has faced and seeks to encourage others to hold fast to these Truths in their own journey of faith.

Jaclyn lives in Raleigh, NC, attends Bob Jones University, and is very active in her local church. Jaclyn's main goal, and the legacy she wants to leave behind is, to be a voice for those with special needs, and to be a faithful servant of her Lord Jesus Christ.